Arthur the Ant
Coloring Book

Janice McLaughlin

ISBN-13: 978-1523652303
ISBN-10: 1523652306

This book belongs to

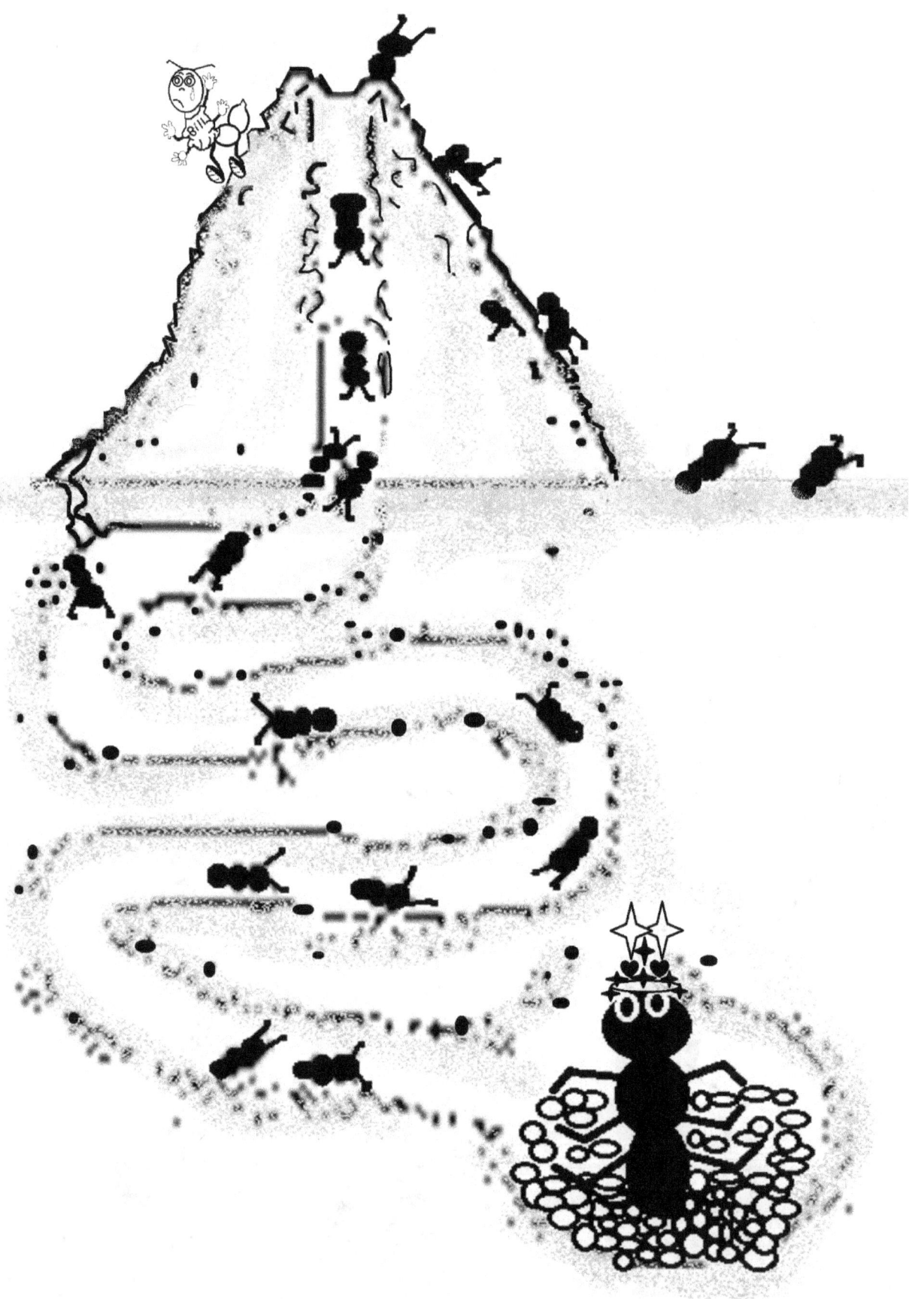

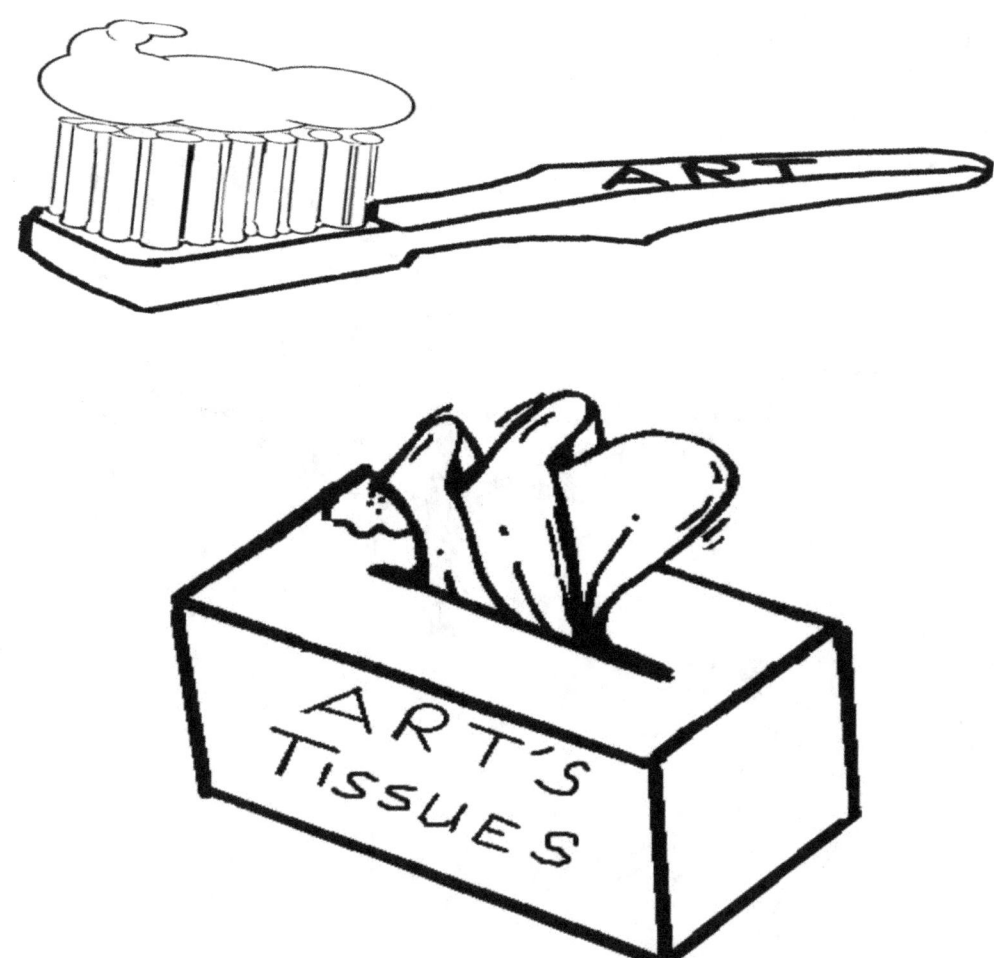

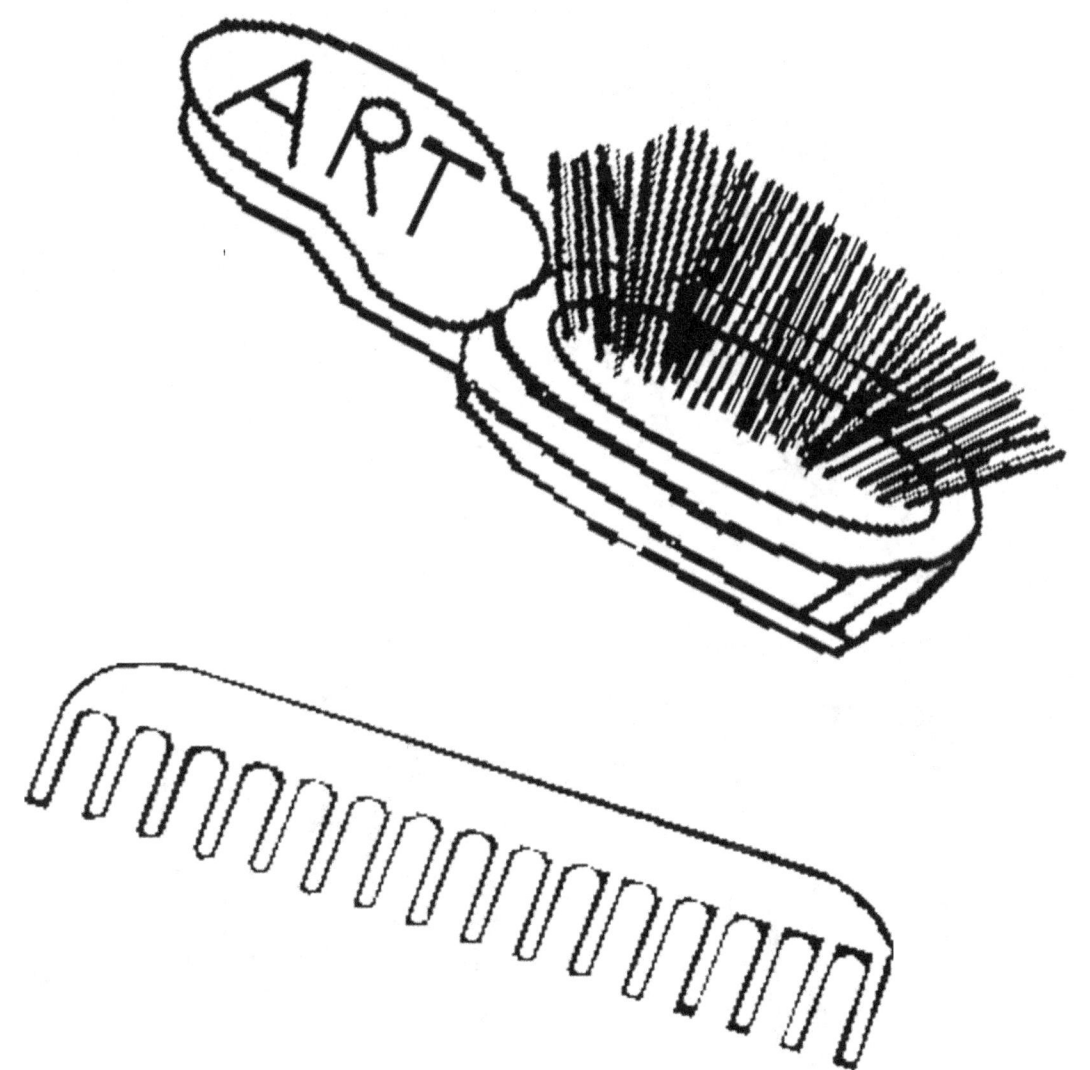

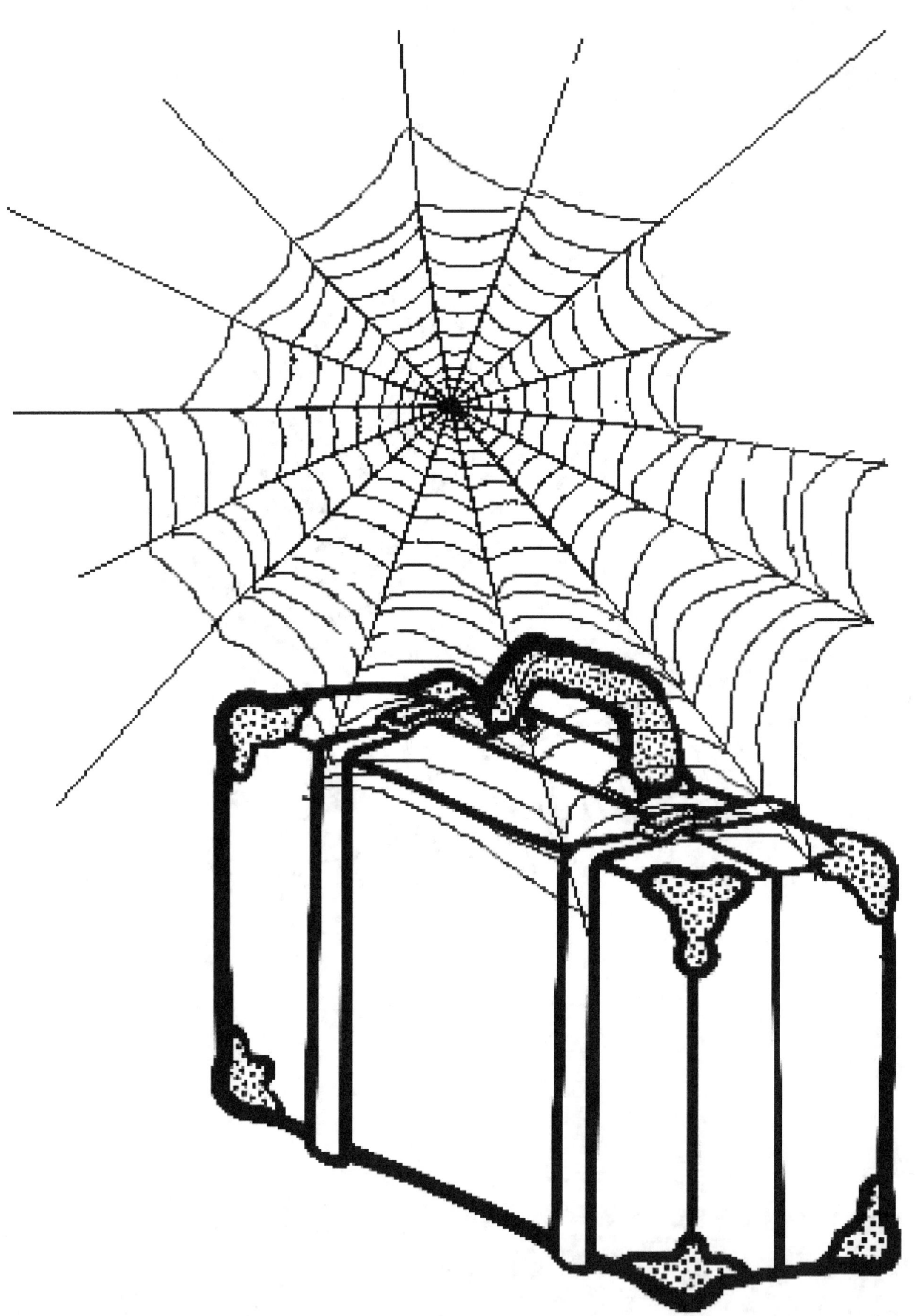

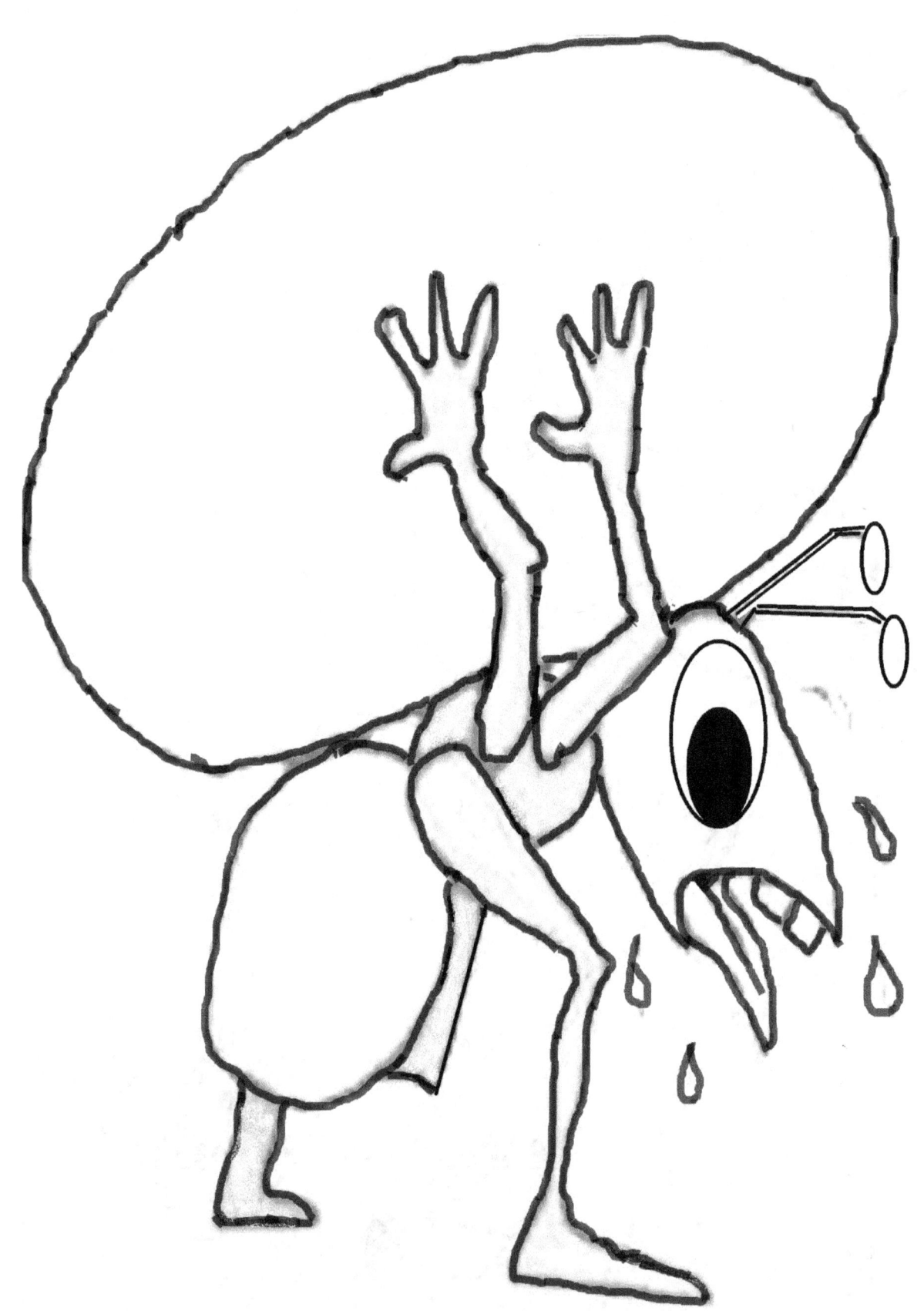

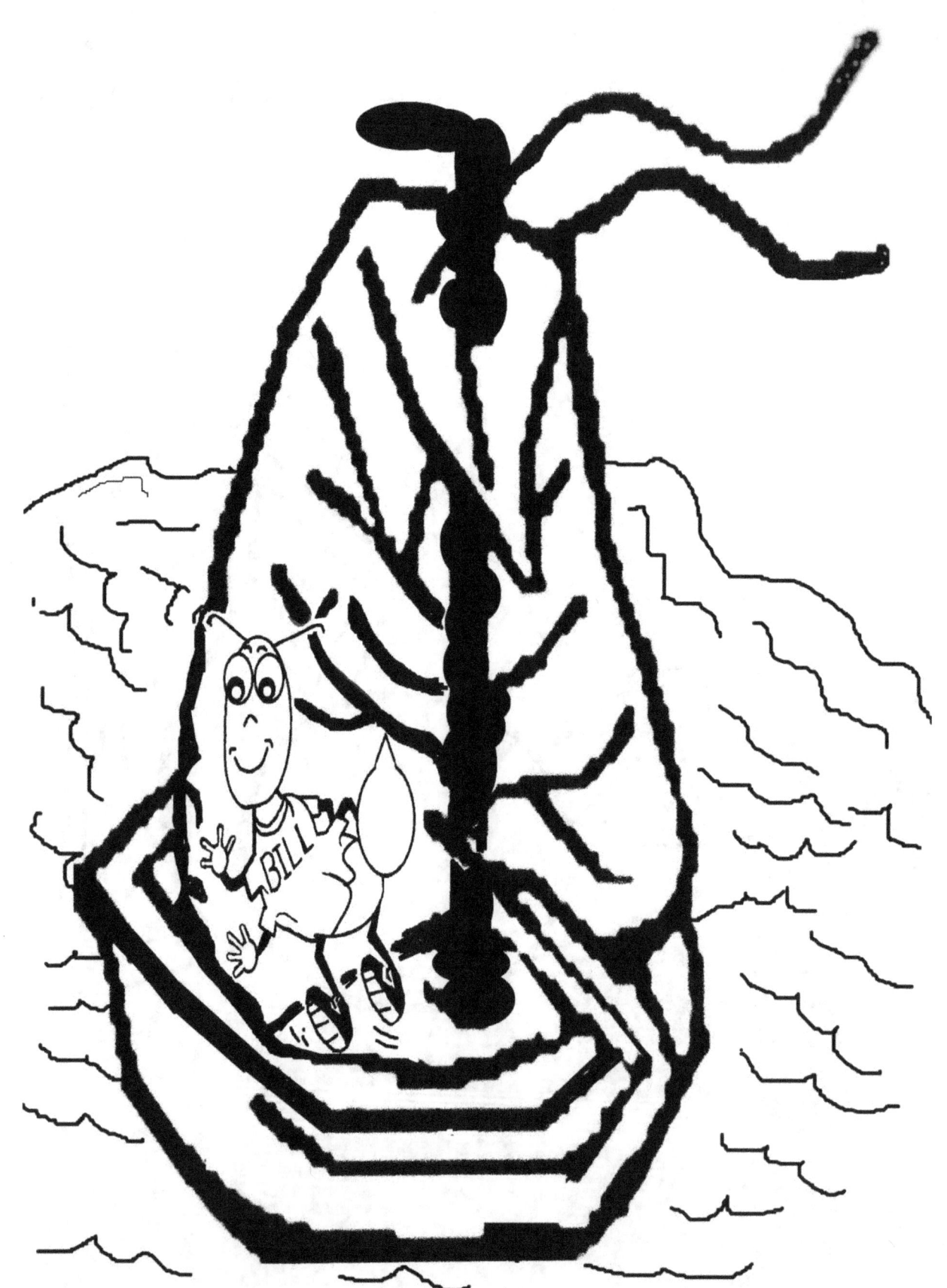

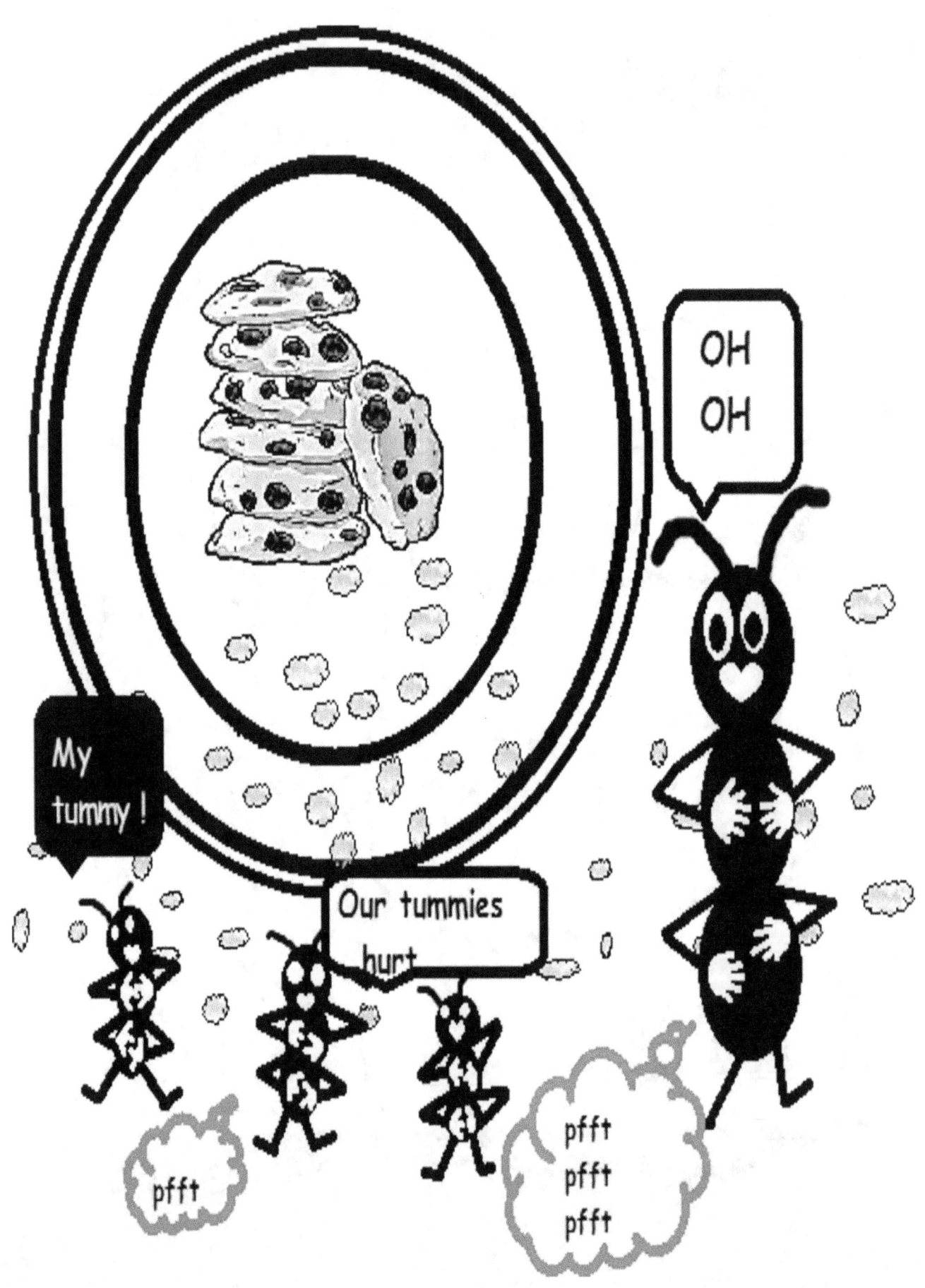

www.ingramcontent.com/pod-product-compliance
Lightning Source LLC
Chambersburg PA
CBHW081537280526
45788CB00010B/3271